Help!
My Anxious Middle Schooler:
Simplified strategies for parents to help break the anxiety cycle

Maria Shkreli, LMHC

First Series: August 2018

Photograph by: Donna Mueller Photography

Printed in the United States of America.

ISBN-13: 978-0-692-16172-2

I would like to say thank you to all the people in my life who have inspired me and stood by me, and to all the kids who work hard to find their strength!

Contents

Chapter 1

Introduction

There are countless books for parents about anxiety — some are complex, some are simple. My goal is to add a simple yet robust option for parents to learn the easy strategies I use in my support groups and individual counseling sessions with middle schoolers, many of which can be used for both teens and adults. The techniques in this book will assist in learning how to identify anxiety and unhealthy thinking patterns in your middle schooler, and how to implement methods to reduce and manage anxiety.

Transitioning from elementary to middle school can trigger stressful emotions in anxious kids. They are now solely responsible for homework, will meet new people, and will share the halls with older students. Additionally, they have to contend with puberty, hormones, drama, being dropped from their elementary school friend groups, fitting in, bullying, and peer pressure. All of this can be incredibly daunting, especially for an anxious kid.

So, what does this mean for parents? First and foremost, you must learn how your middle schooler is feeling. Your role as a parent is critical to your child's progress — it shows them you want to work with them, and the progress potentially made is more successful when parents get involved.

This book isn't written in clinical terms; I don't want to overwhelm you. The strategies and methods you'll discover in the next few pages are a way to start actively helping your middle schooler accept, address, and manage anxiety, helping them work toward a happier and healthier way of coping and thinking.

Use this book as a supplement if you already have a middle schooler in therapy. **If anxiety is severe, professional assistance is your best approach.**

You and your middle schooler will learn:

- To identify triggers of their anxiety episodes
- To identify irrational thoughts and beliefs
- To identify how they feel during an anxiety attack
- To reduce and/or manage their anxiety
- To acknowledge when irrational thinking and/or belief is occurring
- To replace irrational thoughts and beliefs with healthy thoughts and beliefs

I use a form of Cognitive Therapy known as Rational Emotive Behavior Therapy (REBT) to successfully treat adolescents with anxiety disorders. Research has shown this therapy to be highly successful.

REBT alleviates a child's anxiety symptoms by focusing on changing the child's negative thinking. The negative thinking I'm referring to is known as "irrational and/or distorted thinking." The way we think or see things can cause unhealthy behavior. I have organized the chapters in a way that makes it easy for parents and middle schoolers to practice REBT at home.

Chapter 2

Anxiety and the Middle Schooler

I often hear common concerns from parents: Why does Jill worry about tests when she's a good student? Why does Billy worry about the new teacher not liking him? Why is Mary not invited to birthday parties? Why does Pat always complain about being tired? Why does Steph still worry about the style of clothes she wears to school? Why does Adam always get in trouble at school?

Parents and children can suffer emotionally when they don't understand what anxiety is. Anxiety disorders are the most common psychological problems children experience. Anxiety can be either simple or tough to detect in a child, and anxiety becomes a concern when it causes problems. Helping a child becomes easier once a parent understands what's going on.

Anxiety surfaces and magnifies at different stages in life, and middle school has a full array of triggers. Parents also struggle during this unfamiliar, challenging stage, which adds to the anxiety.

Entering middle school presents new challenges of more responsibility, greater independence, increased accountability, and more demanding schoolwork; it is a palpable transition as they go from being little kids directly into adolescence, but are not yet teens. Their hormones are kicking in, and their bodies are changing. All of this means new and more drama.

Middle schoolers who experience low self-esteem struggle to keep friendships alive, are left out of social functions, feel sadness, and eventually withdraw. Not all of them are depressed, but it means they don't know how to work through their anxiety. When they were younger, things may not have bothered them as much because their parents rescued them; they could overlook or hide from certain situations, and they didn't always understand what was going on. Fitting in becomes daunting because they worry about what others think, how they'll be perceived, and what happens when old friends stop being friends.

The addition of social media to middle school life is also wreaking havoc, and it can be a challenge to keep it in balance. Technology is not entirely to blame, but it has a significant role in causing an already anxious kid to be even more anxious. Parents are well aware of the negative impact social media can have on a child. Focus on strengthening your middle schooler's self-esteem, and social media drama will have a minimal impact. Lastly, the potential of being bullied is ever-present.

Unfortunately, bullying in school is a common occurrence, and a middle schooler who is anxious may be more susceptible to being bullied. Why? Because bullies can tell when a middle schooler is trying to fit in, acts different and looks different, and is nervous; a bully knows and targets them. A middle schooler who displays the following has a higher rate of being targeted:

- Lacks assertiveness - they are afraid to speak up
- Lacks close social groups - afraid of being made fun of, afraid of not fitting in
- Lacks self-esteem - afraid to stand up for themselves

What does this have to do with anxiety? Anxious middle schoolers display these symptoms. Bullies know this and they prey on these middle schoolers. So, how do parents help?

Some warning signs may include:

- Not wanting to go to school
- Decline in grades
- Increased sadness
- Increased anxiety
- Not feeling well, stomach aches, headaches, body aches
- Missing personal items - bullies may demand they give them personal items   and/or money
- Trouble sleeping

Bullying can have traumatic effects on middle schoolers, and the pain they experience impacts their daily life. A middle schooler will feel isolated and lonely, and may eventually withdraw socially and from their family.

Effects of bullying include:

- Low self-esteem
- Severe anxiety
- Depression
- Loneliness
- Suicidal thoughts

How to help your middle schooler:

- Learn about bullying
- Learn about the effects of bullying
- Have open discussions with your child
- Encourage your child to tell an adult if they are being bullied. This includes you and/or another trusted adult.

Reiterate to your middle schooler:

- They are valued
- They are strong
- They can be assertive
- They have support - good friends and family
- They don't need to be afraid of telling an adult
- They can be happy

So, how does a parent recognize anxiety? It's not always easy, as other disorders can be present and have similar symptoms, but here are a few examples of how anxiety can manifest in a middle schooler.

Your son has been complaining of stomach aches: When an adolescent feels stressed and/or overwhelmed, physical symptoms may appear.

Your daughter stops hanging out with friends after school: When an adolescent feels stressed and/or overwhelmed, they tend to want to be alone to unwind and don't want to deal with additional stress.

Your son has no homework for a second day or he tells you he did it in school: Adolescents lie to avoid confrontation.

Your son has been acting up in class and is not paying attention: Anxiety can cause poor concentration.

The following are common anxiety symptoms a middle schooler may display:
- Poor concentration
- Low self-esteem
- Sadness or depression
- Complaining most of the time
- Lack of motivation, laziness
- Lack of follow-through with schoolwork and chores
- Poor grades - struggles with homework
- Lack of classroom participation
- Social issues, including peer issues
- Avoids participating in school activities such as sports

What parents need to remember:
- Middle school is very different from elementary school
- Over time, your middle schooler is going to change
- Importance of talking about:
  - puberty and hormonal changes
  - the fears they have
  - peer pressure
  - self-esteem
  - Bullying
  - new classes, getting to class on time, new routines, and new teachers

How to work with an anxious middle schooler:

- **Help and teach your middle schooler to manage their anxiety.**

- **Be a positive influence on their fears and insecurities** - let them know they can come to you with their fears, and that you want them to share if they are being excluded from friend groups or being bullied; validate their feelings.

- **Don't project your own anxiety onto your child** - Don't make your child more anxious. If you are afraid of something, let them know, and if they are afraid, ask them to share it with you. Avoiding situations that cause anxiety can lead to an endless cycle.

- **Don't ask questions that make them more anxious** - you may ask, "How are you and your friends doing?" This type of open-ended question can cause a middle schooler to question why you are asking, and they will start to worry that you know something they don't know. Asking, "Are you and your friends okay?" leads to an answer that your child can answer directly - they don't wander to "Worry Land."

- **Teach your child how to tolerate their anxiety and recognize triggers** - Teach them self-talk - yes, how to talk in their heads. When they find they are anxious, have them ask themselves, "Why do I feel anxious? I know I am anxious, but I will be fine, because I can be." This is the opposite of what anxious middle schoolers usually do. Most of the time, they automatically self-talk with negative thoughts. The goal is to teach self-talk with positivity.

In the next several pages, you will find the most common anxiety disorders along with brief descriptions. After you've read the next chapter, think about your middle schooler and find the diagnosis that relates closest to the symptoms you've noticed.

Chapter 3

The Major Types of Anxiety

- Generalized Anxiety Disorder
- Panic Disorder
- Agoraphobia
- Other Phobias
- Social Anxiety Disorder
- Separation Anxiety Disorder
- Obsessive-Compulsive Disorder

The difference between normal anxiety and an anxiety disorder is when the anxiety affects one's quality of life. Listed below are steps that parents can take to help your anxious middle schooler:

- ➤ Know the specific type of anxiety they have
- ➤ Help them accept their anxiety
- ➤ Help them manage their anxiety
- ➤ Help them understand the causes and triggers of their anxiety
- ➤ Seek professional help if the anxiety is severe
- ➤ Join a parent support group
- ➤ Join your middle schooler in a support group

Generalized Anxiety Disorder is when an individual has excessive worry about events or activities, e.g., family, school, friends, or poor grades. These feelings occur most of the time with no specific trigger. This anxiety is difficult to control and is disproportionate to the fear.

Common symptoms include:
- Sleep disturbance
- Irritability
- Difficulty concentrating
- Muscle tension
- Exertion or fatigue
- Restlessness
- Chronic headaches

Panic Disorder is when an individual experiences uncontrollable, recurrent episodes of panic and fear within minutes of each other. There is no warning before the panic attacks occur and they're not always linked to a trigger, making them difficult to predict.

Common symptoms include:
- Pounding heart
- Shortness of breath
- Nausea
- Dizziness, lightheadedness
- Fear of losing control
- Numbness
- Chills
- Sweating
- Choking feeling
- Trembling
- Feeling detached from reality

Separation Anxiety Disorder is an individual's excessive worry about being away from their parents. The individual fears that something will happen to their parents and that they will never see them again. This is often seen in children, but also appears in adolescents when a stressor has occurred.

Common symptoms include:
- Extreme distress when separated from home or the attachment figure
- Persistent fear of being alone
- Frequent physical complaints while separated from the attachment figure

Obsessive-Compulsive Disorder is a condition involving obsessions and/or compulsions. The individual's disturbing obsessions or compulsions (some individuals have both) impact daily life; they may spend an hour a day on such behaviors. Obsessions may include fear of germs; compulsions may include repetitive behaviors of washing hands.

Common symptoms:

Obsessions include:

- Continuous thoughts that cause distress. Attempts to ignore the thoughts, urges, images, and reasons that lead to the compulsive behavior
- Unfounded suspicion of individuals
- Need for orderliness
- Need for cleanliness; fear of germs

Compulsions:

- Repetitive behaviors which the individual feels inclined to perform in response to an obsession
- Repetitive behaviors include: washing of hands, performing a certain task a specific number of times, or checking appliances a specific number of times
- Behaviors are aimed at reducing anxiety and distress, or preventing a feared event

Social Anxiety Disorder is an individual's persistent fear of social situations, or a situation where the individual may need to perform.

Common symptoms include:

- Fear of meeting other people
- Easily embarrassed
- Feeling insecure and out of place
- Fear of having to speak in public
- Fear of being the center of attention
- Fear of being criticized

Agoraphobia is when an individual is anxious about being outside of the home or in open places. The fear is having a panic attack when leaving home, not a fear of people.

Common symptoms:

- Fear of being outside the home
- Fear of public transportation
- Fear of enclosed/open places
- Fear of inability to escape when needed

Other Phobias include:

- Arachnophobia - fear of spiders
- Ophidiophobia - fear of snakes
- Acrophobia - fear of heights
- Cynophobia - fear of dogs

Chapter 4

How do you Communicate?

A sample conversation between a mother and her eighth grade son:

Mother: (*In a loud, firm tone*) You have to do well because you'll be a failure without good grades.

Son: That's all you care about. You don't understand what it's like.

Mother: I was once your age, and I do understand! I didn't have all that you have today. Life is easy for you. All I ask is that you do well in school. I don't get you.

They continue for a bit until the therapist interrupts and suggests they take a deep breath. The therapist tells the mom to look at her son and ask him to tell her what he meant by, "you don't understand." The son begins to explain, but three minutes into the conversation, the mother interrupts. The therapist signals for the mother to stop and asks her to let her son explain without interruption. In turn, the therapist tells the son to ask the mother why she feels the way she does about his grades, and as she starts to explain, the son interrupts. The therapist signals for the son to stop and asks him to hold his comments until his mom has finished.

What's going on here? Neither mother nor son was listening to each other, and each was getting annoyed. The son became irritable, started fidgeting, and asked to leave because he was tired. The son's anxiety exhausted him, and because he didn't have coping skills to manage the anxiety, he shut down, which frustrated the mom; it appeared that her son was neither caring nor listening. They both felt they were doing their best; however, they were creating tension - two frustrated individuals with no solution to the issue. So, the goal is to learn how to be both a good listener and good communicator.

Half of you, most likely, recently experienced that same scenario, and the other half had a similar experience.

Not to worry; effective listening and communication are not always easy. There are many factors that go into miscommunication, including feeling shy, scared, or angry, all of which break down effective communication. Additionally, many cultures view an adolescent "talking back" as a sign of disrespect. An adolescent whose parents grew up in a different culture and/or country may struggle with mixed signals, as their friends communicate differently with their parents. Furthermore, different genders often communicate differently. Boys tend to internalize because they may have been taught to not express emotions, and girls may be apprehensive because they tend to be more sensitive.

The inability to listen, and its associated complications, can also cause distress in family situations that would easily be handled if we knew how to better communicate with each other. Complications may include: differences in learning styles, cultural differences, and psychological disorders. The following questions will help you determine where you stand with regard to your listening and communication skills.

Take a moment to answer the following questions:

- When is the last time you sat down with your middle schooler and talked *with* them?
  _____

- Do you know which kind of music they listen to? If so, do you know *why* they like it?_____

- Do they have new interests? _____

- Which kinds of television shows do they like? *Why* do they like them?
  _____

- What do they like about themselves, and why?
  _____

- If they could change something about themselves, what would it be?
  _____

- How do they feel about the relationship they have with you ?
  _____

- Do they trust you? _____

- Are they afraid of you? If so, have you ever asked why?
  _____

If you've never asked any of these questions, don't worry, it's not too late. Check in with yourself and decide whether you're ready to work on changing your own behaviors and actions. If you answered yes, then continue.

Tips to starting a new communication relationship with your middle schooler:

1. **Start over:** Beating yourself up over past mistakes is pointless, so instead, move forward. Take care of your "stuff." If you have anger issues, are anxious, or have distorted thinking - seek professional help so that you can move to a better place for yourself and your middle schooler.

2. **Learn how to engage in active listening:** Understand the information, including the words and emotions your middle schooler is trying to communicate - it shows them you are interested and engaged in the conversation. Also, provide positive feedback. When your middle schooler speaks, let them speak without interrupting. You will have your turn once they finish, and let your middle schooler know that the same applies to them when you are talking.

3. **Learn how to validate how they feel:** Don't disqualify how they feel; they're trying their best to work through their stuff. You are an adult and have experienced life, whereas they are just starting and need your caring guidance.

4. **Don't expect them to be you:** Perhaps you were a great athlete, or a ballerina, or a great student. If you expect them to be at least as good or better than you were, it hurts them. They are doing their best. Accept what they are good at, and not what you want them to be good at. Parents who believe they can change their kids, often have an unhappy middle schooler who is just doing what you want, instead of what they want, and this is stressful for a "kid." They will shine once they feel accepted by you.

5. **Learn that being calm is always productive**: You may want to jump out of your skin, you may want to yell, but these actions resolve nothing. Not only will you scare them, but you are also teaching them to react the same way. Nonverbal signals include facial expressions and body language. When you speak, try to match your words to your nonverbal signals. Remember, they follow by example. If you want them to be calm and rational, you'll have to be calm and rational. It will be difficult in the beginning, but once this becomes the norm, your child's irrational thoughts and behaviors will change for the better.

6. **Share wisely with your child:** You were once their age. Remember how you felt when your parents shared their stories with you? It was cool, boring, and interesting, all at once. Work on not making your middle schooler feel like you're being judgmental or condescending. Let them know you understand that their childhood is different, that they can share their experiences with you, to help you better understand them.

7. **Lectures are a major no-no:** Middle schoolers do not listen to people who lecture them. How many times have you found yourself rolling your eyes when you were lectured to? It's no different for a middle schooler. Often, when parents lecture, it is hostile and filled with "should've, could've, why, and how." Too much information is being relayed, and your middle schooler can shut down. Further, a middle schooler is not mature enough to understand what you are trying to accomplish by lecturing.

Word choices and other ways parents can communicate with their middle schoolers:

1. **Learn to use "I" statements**: "I am hurt when this happens. I am unsure how to help you. I want you to tell me what that feels like. I want you to trust me. I am here for you when you need me. I don't understand, so help me understand. I will listen to you. I may get angry, but I will calm down— this happens at times because I'm learning how to deal with situations I don't know how to deal with."

2. **Avoid "You" statements**. Be very careful here: "You are always late for school. You never listen when I tell you to do something. You always forget to clean your room. You don't know how to do that. You don't try hard enough." These statements are negative reinforcements. You don't want to have a middle schooler who believes they aren't good, smart, efficient, etc.

3. **Avoid blaming** your child.

4. **Learn to use the 10 second rule.** If you feel angry, let your child know that you're going to take a 10 second break before you talk to them. If you're still angry, let your child know you need a few minutes to gather your thoughts.

5. **Ask** them how they feel.

6. **Ask** them what they think.

7. **Ask** their opinion.

8. **Ask** them to come up with solutions.

9. **Ask** them to come up with consequences.

10. **Set up a structure** with them, and let them be a part of the process. Kids want and need structure.

11. **Follow through**. *This is very important*. This is where most of the progress fails. If you don't follow through, you also teach your middle schooler to not follow through.

Example of ineffective communication and listening:

Cathy is entering the seventh grade. She has always done well in school, and has many friends. She participates in sports and is part of a dance group. Cathy's grades, however, have started to decline, and she's having problems with her friend group. She begins to complain about the kids in school and one of her teachers. She isn't sleeping well, and she's getting up late for school.

Mom: Hi, Cathy. How was school today?
Cathy: It was okay. Gotta go to my room; talk to you later.

An hour later, Mom knocks on Cathy's door.

Mom: Are you finished with your homework?
Cathy: No, not yet, talking with some friends. I'll start my homework in a few minutes.

Mom notices Cathy is distracted.

Mom: Are you okay, Cathy?
Cathy: Sure, Mom, I'm good.

The next day, the school counselor calls Mom and tells her Cathy's grades are dropping, and teachers have noticed she's been eating lunch alone.

Mom: Hi, Cathy. How was school today?
Cathy: Stupid. Middle School is stupid.

Mom: I received a call from your guidance counselor and we talked about your grades and how you've been eating alone.
Cathy: Yeah, my friends are stupid. School is hard and I'm getting all confused with the homework.

Mom: Girls can be mean. Just ignore them. What's going on with your grades? Do you need a tutor for school? If you do, let me know and I'll look into it for you. For now, no phone use until your grades get better.

Cathy: That's not fair. What if my friends text me and I miss something?
Mom: It's not the end of the world if you don't text them back. Do some reading - you need to get your grades back up.

Example of effective communication and listening:

Mom: Hi, Cathy. How how are you?
Cathy: I'm okay. Gotta go to my room; talk to you later.

Mom: Hold on, sweetie, can we catch up for a few minutes and then you can go up to your room?
Cathy: Okay, I guess I have a few minutes. Why, is something wrong?

Mom: Nothing is wrong, It's just that we are so busy all the time and I want to hear how things are going and share a funny story with you.
Cathy: Okay. School was the same. Nothing interesting. Oh, wait, John got hit by a book today and broke his nose. Tracy got into a fight with her best friend and they called each other some bad names.

Mom: Goodness, that's a busy day. How did you feel about all of this?
Cathy: It's school, it's drama, it doesn't affect me because they are aren't in my group. Anyway, I'm going up to my room now.

The next day, the school counselor calls Mom and tells her Cathy's grades are dropping, and teachers have noticed she's been eating lunch alone.

Mom: Hi, Cathy. How are you? How was your day?
Cathy: Stupid. Middle School is stupid.

Mom: I'm sorry you're feeling this way. I received a call from your guidance counselor and we talked about your grades and how you've been eating alone.
Cathy: Yeah, my friends are stupid. School is hard and I'm getting all confused with the homework.

Mom: Cathy, I can't tell you that this stuff won't happen, and that you won't be hurt, but I can tell you that worrying about it can affect you in unhealthy ways. How about this - settle in, have a snack, rest a while, and when you're ready we can sit together and talk about what your going through and how it's making you feel. If you like, I'll share some of my experiences in life if it'll help you understand things a little better. I'm going to leave the choice up to you, let me know.

Cathy: I like that plan, mom. Thanks. Let me just rest and do a few things.

Practice:

Jim is a very smart sixth grader at his middle school. He is being bullied during lunch and is afraid to tell anyone. Lately, he has been doing poorly in school and started acting out because he's afraid that the other kids will think he's a wimp. On Tuesday, Jim had a fight during art class and ended up at the principal's office. The school called his mother to tell her about the incident.

Ineffective communication response:

Mom: Hi, Jim. I heard what happened at school.

Jim: I hate the kids in school. They are so mean. If they weren't so mean, I wouldn't have had to throw my clay project at them.

Mom: Who is bullying you? What happened?

Jim: Steve. He wasn't always mean to me. I don't understand why he is now.

Mom: Steve is not a good kid. I will call his parents and talk to them.

Jim: Okay, Mom. You tell the parents how mean he is. I'm not going to school tomorrow, I want to take a day off.

Mom: Okay, Jim, stay home and rest. I'll let the school know you'll make up detention .

Write an effective communication response:

Mom:

Jim:

Mom:

Jim:

Mom:

Chapter 5

What is Irrational Thinking?

Ask yourself, "How often does your middle schooler find find fault in everyone else? Is it almost all of the time, or just some of the time?" If it's almost all the time, it is likely affecting their quality of life. Now, ask yourself how it can be *all of the time*. Is everyone else always wrong? Do people always wrong them?

The goal is to recognize your middle schoolers' thinking patterns and to remind them when their thoughts are irrational. "Why are they thinking this way? What do are they looking to gain by thinking this way? How do they feel when they think this way?" Once your middle schooler begins to recognize irrational thoughts, they will start to think in a healthier way.

On the next page, you will find common irrational thinking patterns. After you have read each one, determine those that apply to your middle schooler. Check them off and date the bottom of the page. Your goal is to help your middle schooler recognize irrational thinking patterns and to help replace them with healthier ones. Occasionally, revisit the irrational thinking checklist to see how far your middle schooler has come. It's great to see the progress they're making.

Irrational Thinking Patterns

❏   **All-or-nothing thinking:** An individual views everything in the extreme. It's either right or wrong, true or untrue. Rarely does one see shades of grey. This is the inability to see alternatives to a problem.

❏   **Overgeneralization:** An individual takes one experience and believes this will always occur. For example, you're not invited to a party, therefore you'll never be invited to any parties.

❏   **Catastrophizing or minimizing:** An individual either exaggerates or minimizes a situation. For example:
  Catastrophizing: Billy bumped into another student during lunch and the student's apple fell on the floor. The student tells Billy it's okay and that it's just an accident, but Billy gets so upset over it that he thinks about it for days.
  Minimizing: Mary beat the track record at school and won an award. Afterward, she gave a short speech and people applauded her. However, Mary complained that she was so nervous that her speech was dumb.

❏   **Emotional reasoning:** An individual views that how they feel is what defines them. For example, Jane feels dumb, so she's convinced that she is dumb, even though she does well in school.

❏   **"Should" statement:** This statement (also includes "ought" or "must") usually induces feelings of guilt; the motivation for doing something is based on what others think. This thinking usually leads to procrastination.

Irrational Thinking Patterns

❑ **Labeling and mislabeling:** An individual does the opposite of overgeneralization. Labeling - you label yourself: "I'm dumb." Mislabeling - you label someone else's behavior: "She's a weirdo."

❑ **Personalization:** An individual believes they're the cause of a negative event. For example, if Mary doesn't call you back, she must not like you.

❑ **Fortune-telling:** An individual tends to predict that things will turn out badly.

❑ **Disqualifying the positives:** An individual doesn't give themselves credit when they do something positive and/or good. They feel it's not deserved.

❑ **Negative thoughts:** An individual only looks at the negative side of an event, situation, or action. For example, you lost your lunch money, but you had a great day with friends. Your focus is on the lost money.

I have added this checklist at the end of the book for you to hang on the refrigerator and/or in your middle schooler's room. It's a reminder to check in with the irrational thinking.

What irrational thinking/behavior looks like:

Thoughts affect both your feelings and your body sensations, which, in turn, affect your overall behavior towards situations.

For example, thinking, "nobody likes me" can create a feeling of anxiety (feelings) around other kids, which, in turn, may cause headaches (bodily sensations) resulting in withdrawing from your friends (behavior), resulting in feeling left out.

Thoughts

"Nobody Likes me"
"I always make mistakes""

Behavior

Withdraw from friends
Stop doing what you enjoy

Feelings

Sad
Anxious

Body Sensations
No energy
Tired
Tense

On the next page, you will find a practice situation to work on. Try to look at the situation with your new thinking and behavior. Once you're comfortable with the techniques you've learned, you're on your way to learning and using REBT.

Practice by redoing this scenario with healthy thinking. How would you approach the situation?

Situation: Kristen is invited to a birthday party by a girl from her science class.

Negative Thought: "I won't know anyone at this party and I'll just be out of place. She probably invited me because I'm the 'boring' girl."

Emotion: Anxious

Behavior: Kristen lies and tells her friend she already has plans for the night.

What is the new, positive, rational thought:

Situation: Steve notices that a girl in class keeps looking at him.

Negative Thought: "Do I have something on my face? Is my fly down? Do I look bad? I need to go to the bathroom and check."

Emotion: Self-conscious and anxious

Behavior: Steve avoids the girl and jets off to the bathroom.

What is the new, rational behavior:

CHAPTER 6

Teach Your Middle Schooler to Worry Less

This might be a challenge, and your child may be reluctant because they may be shy or embarrassed to share their worries. People are generally afraid of feeling or being vulnerable. For now, the focus is still on you, as you learn how to understand this information and prepare to implement it at home. You should use an event that you've noticed your middle schooler has already experienced or is currently experiencing, and fill in an anxiety scale log for them. Record several incidents; determine whether you've used the techniques you've learned so far. If you haven't, reread the chapters where you think you're unsure. If you have done a good job, you're a step closer to learning REBT.

Thought-stopping:

Your last step before moving onto REBT is brief and self-explanatory. Each time you notice your child's irrational thinking, you will ask them to stop and think about the thought: "Why are you anxious; what is your thinking?" After repeatedly invoking this method, your middle schooler will learn to do it on their own. Filling out the blank worksheets in Chapter 8 will reinforce all the techniques that they've learned.

Once they get the hang of it, they won't need the worksheets. They will automatically stop, *recall* the worksheets, and think internally before letting the anxiety take control. The next two pages contain examples of how to use the worksheets.

Anxiety Scale

It's Sunday evening. Jessica is watching television when she starts to think about tomorrow's math test.

Level of anxiety experienced:
Scale of 1 - 10 (1 being the least anxious; 10 being the most)

    ✓   8

What was the trigger: Test at school tomorrow.

Your anxious thoughts: Too much information to learn, don't have enough time to study, my parents will be mad at me.

Your anxious behaviors: Tried to listen to music to calm my fears, but still worried about failing the test.

Which symptoms did you experience:

- ✓ Irritability
- ❏ Muscle tension
- ❏ Unable to sleep
- ✓ Difficulty concentrating
- ❏ Tired
- ✓ Restlessness
- ❏ Headaches
- ❏ Persistent worry about things that are out of proportion to the event
- ✓ Overthinking
- ❏ Indecisiveness
- ✓ Inability to not worry
- ✓ Trembling
- ❏ Nervousness
- ❏ Sweating

Anxiety Scale

Jack texted Dave at 10:30 Wednesday night. Jack waited, and eventually, Dave texted back, "Give me ten minutes." But Dave never got back to Jack.

Level of anxiety experienced:
Scale of 1 - 10 (1 being the least anxious; 10 being the most)

   ✓   9

What was the trigger: Dave didn't text me back when he said he would.

Your anxious thoughts: Maybe he doesn't want to talk to me; maybe he is mad at me. Maybe he doesn't want to hang out after school.

Your anxious behaviors: Kept texting my friend - texted and called at least twelve times.

Which symptoms did you experience:

- ✓ Irritability
- ❑ Muscle tension
- ✓ Unable to sleep
- ✓ Difficulty concentrating
- ❑ Tired
- ✓ Restlessness
- ❑ Headaches
- ✓ Persistent worry about things that are out of proportion to the event
- ✓ Overthinking
- ❑ Indecisiveness
- ✓ Inability to not worry
- ❑ Trembling
- ✓ Nervousness
- ❑ Sweating

Now we are ready to put all this together and help your anxious middle schooler. The next chapter will teach you how to use REBT.

Chapter 7

Welcome to REBT

What is Rational Emotive Behavior Therapy (REBT)?

REBT is a type of cognitive-behavioral therapy developed by Albert Ellis. Ellis' research concluded that people are not affected by events that occur, but rather, by their view of the event. REBT addresses the underlying reason for an individual's irrational thoughts/beliefs. It focuses on helping individuals learn that the way they think ("cognitive") and act ('behavioral") about the problems or situations, affects how they both feel and react. This therapy is also viewed as confrontational, as it reminds an individual that they're responsible for the way they think; people find it difficult to believe they can change their thinking. In therapy, individuals learn the technique and, with practice, make positive changes, recognizing how their view is affecting the situation that caused the irrational thinking.

The goal of REBT is to help the individual with the following:

- Learn to recognize their irrational thinking
- Learn the triggers that cause the anxiety
- Learn how to challenge their irrational thoughts
- Learn coping skills
- Learn positive thoughts and beliefs
- Learn how to decrease and or manage their anxiety
- Learn how to safely face the situation causing the anxiety
- Learn how they behave in the situations that cause anxiety

"The outcome of REBT is to change B"

A = the **Activating** event/experience
B = the **Belief** about (or interpretation of) the experience
C = the upsetting emotional **Consequences**
D = **Disputing** of irrational ideas
E = new emotional consequence or **Effect**

How REBT Works

Example 1:

A = the **Activating** event/experience: something that happens.

My friends didn't invite me to the movies.

B = the **Belief** about (or interpretation of) the experience of an event.

I'm a loser, not fun to be around, so I'd be boring at the party.

C = the upsetting, emotional **Consequences**: the emotional, behavioral, cognitive consequences of your beliefs of **B**.

I feel sad. I am a loser. They don't like me. I just won't go to the movies.

D = the **Disputing** of irrational ideas: find the evidence of how **B** will affect your life.

I am fun, so my friends probably forgot to invite me. I have other friends that invite me to the movies; I know they like me.

E = the new emotional consequence or **Effect**: learn appropriate emotion for **C**.

I just want to have fun with my friends; if they aren't good friends and intentionally didn't invite me, I have other friends who I can be with.

Example 2:

A = the **Activating** event/experience: something that happens.

John failed his math test.

B = the **Belief** about (or interpretation of) the experience of an event.

John believes he has to have good grades, otherwise he's dumb.

C = the upsetting emotional **Consequences:** the emotional, behavioral, cognitive consequences of your beliefs of **B**.

John is depressed because of his bad grade.

D = the **Disputing** of irrational ideas: find the evidence of how **B** will affect your life.

Where is the belief that you are dumb because you failed one test?

E = the new emotional consequence or **Effect**: learn appropriate emotion for **C**.

John is sad that he failed his math test, but the test was one of the most difficult this year. Failing does not make him dumb.

Practice the use of REBT

Apply a current situation:

A = the **Activating** event/experience. Something that is happening:

_____

B = the **Belief** about (or interpretation of) your experience of the event:

_____

C = the upsetting emotional **Consequences.** The emotional, behavioral, cognitive consequences of your beliefs of **B**:

_____

D = the **Disputing** of irrational ideas. Find the evidence of how **B** will affect your life:

_____

E = the new emotional consequence or **Effect.** Learn appropriate emotion for **C**:

_____

Practice the use of REBT

Apply a past situation:

A = the **Activating** event/experience. Something that happened:

_____

B = the **Belief** about (or interpretation of) your experience of the event:

_____

C = the upsetting emotional **Consequences.** The emotional, behavioral, cognitive consequences of your beliefs of **B**:

_____

D = the **Disputing** of irrational ideas. Find the evidence of how **B** will affect your life:

_____

E = the new emotional consequence or **Effect**. Learn appropriate emotion for **C**:

_____

CHAPTER 8

Implementing The Plan

It is now time for you to implement the tools and skills you've learned. The goal is for your middle schooler to learn to accept their anxiety and irrational thinking, and also learn the steps to take to reduce and manage their anxiety.

I've made the exercises short and easy to follow to keep your middle schooler engaged. *Good luck!*

Reminder

Stay calm when talking to them
Use your 10 second rule, if needed
Use "I" statements
Listen to them
Pay attention to your body language, facial expressions, and tone
Ask their opinion
Give them choices
Respect their feelings

Your Middle Schooler's Turn.

Ask your middle schooler to complete the following tree. Once completed, talk with them about it. Ask them about how they answered the questions.

The First Tree: Draw and describe how anxiety feels to you.

STEP 1. Think about *you*. STEP 2. Each leaf you place on this tree will represent a symptom you feel. STEP 3. Severe symptoms will be closer to the top of the tree; less severe symptoms will be closer to the bottom. STEP 4. Make it interesting; use colored pens or pencils to distinguish severity/symptoms. STEP 5. Once completed, think about the following: How does the tree look and feel to you? How does the tree make you feel?

Ask your middle schooler to complete the following tree. Once completed, talk with them about the difference between tree one and two.

Second Tree: Draw and describe how *you would feel* with no anxiety.

All About Me

Write and/or draw the answers to the following questions:

What I love about me:

What I'm good at:

What scares me:

What I worry about the most:

When do I feel the most anxious:

What do I do when I'm anxious:

Stop those thoughts

We sometimes think about negative things over and over again – this is unhealthy thinking. You can stop this by *recognizing* when you're repeating the negative thinking in your head. Date the bottom of the page.

List the negative thoughts you repeat over and over.

Date:_____

Log: Learning about your Worries

Upsetting events don't happen as often as you think, but when they do, they can cause kids to feel afraid, upset, and helpless. There are different kinds of upsetting/confusing events. Let's learn about the anxiety-inducing events that you experience.

When does it happen?

Why does it happen?

How often does it happen?

How do you feel when it happens?

How do you handle the event?

Your "Anxiety Scale"

Level of anxiety you experienced:

What was the trigger:

Your anxious thoughts:

Your anxious behaviors:

Which symptoms did you experience:

- ❏ Irritability
- ❏ Muscle tension
- ❏ Unable to sleep
- ❏ Difficulty concentrating
- ❏ Tired
- ❏ Restlessness
- ❏ Headaches
- ❏ Persistent worry about things that are out of proportion to the event
- ❏ Overthinking
- ❏ Indecisiveness
- ❏ Inability to not worry
- ❏ Trembling
- ❏ Nervousness
- ❏ Sweating

Coping with your upsetting feelings

When you experience an upsetting feeling, there are steps you can take to reduce the intensity. What are some things you do, and could do, to reduce the feelings?

What you do:

What you can do instead:

Remember, you are in charge of your feelings.

What are my goals in reducing and/or managing my anxiety?

Goal # 1:

Goal completed: Date_____

Goal #2:

Goal completed: Date_____

Goal #3:

Goal completed: Date_____

Practice your ABC

 Activating Event

 Belief

 Emotional Consequence

Date:_____

Irrational Thinking Patterns

❑   **All-or-nothing thinking:** An individual views everything in the extreme. It's either right or wrong, true or untrue. Rarely does one see shades of grey. This is the inability to see alternatives to a problem.

❑   **Overgeneralization:** An individual takes one experience and believes this will always occur. For example, you're not invited to a party, therefore you'll never be invited to any parties.

❑   **Catastrophizing or minimizing:** An individual either exaggerates or minimizes a situation. For example:
    Catastrophizing: Billy bumped into another student during lunch, and the student's apple fell on the floor. The student tells Billy that it's okay and that it's just an accident, but Billy gets so upset he thinks about it for days.
    Minimizing: Mary beat the track record at school and won an award. Afterward, she gave a short speech and people applauded her. However, Mary complained that she was nervous about her speech being dumb.

❑   **Emotional reasoning:** An individual views how they feel as what defines them. For example, Jane feels dumb, so she's convinced that she is, even though she does well in school.

❑   **"Should" statement:** This statement (also includes "ought" or "must") usually induces feelings of guilt, as the motivation for doing something is based on what others think. This thinking usually leads to procrastination.

❑   **Labeling and mislabeling:** An individual who does the opposite of overgeneralization. Labeling - you label yourself: "I'm dumb." Mislabeling - you label someone else's behavior "She's a weirdo."

❑   **Personalization:** An individual believes they're the cause of a negative event. For example, if Mary doesn't call you back, she must not like you.

❑   **Fortune-telling:** An individual tends to predict that things will turn out badly.

❑   **Disqualifying the positives:** An individual doesn't give themselves credit when they do some positive and/or good. They feel it's not deserved.

❑   **Negative thoughts:** An individual only looks at the negative side of an event, situation, or action. For example, you lost your lunch money, but you had a great day with friends. Your focus is on the lost money.

In conclusion: Parents, Remember

- Ask your child how they feel, emotionally and physically
- Listen without interrupting your child when they speak

- Ask your child how they can handle a situation
- Ask your child how you can help
- Teach your child to be accountable for choices they make, and to understand the consequences
- Remind your child that you are there for them
- Tell your child you may not be able to relate, but you will try to understand
- Tell your child, "We can get through this together as a family."

- Being a kid is tough
- Kids need to be kids
- Kids are not adults
- Kids need to know they can trust you
- ***Remind them they are in control of their thoughts, feelings, emotions and behaviors.***

Most important; hugs and kisses never grow old!

References

American Psychiatric Association, Diagnostic and Statistical Manual for Mental Disorders, DSM-5 (2013). APA Press; 5th Edition

Corcoran & Fisher (2000). *Measures for Clinical* Practice: A Sourcebook. 3rd Edition. Free Press

Corcoran & Fisher (2007). *Measures for Clinical Practice and Research*: A Sourcebook. NY, NY; Oxford University Press

Curran, L. A. (2013). *101 trauma-informed interventions: Activities, exercises and assignments for moving the client and therapy forward.* Eau Claire, WI: PESI.

Drummond, R. Jones, K. (2009). *Assessment Procedures for Counselors and Helping Professionals*, 7th Edition. Prentice Hall

Dryden, W. (2015). *Reason to change: A rational emotive behaviour therapy (rebt) workbook.* Routledge

Ellis, A., & Joffe-Ellis, D. (2011). *Rational emotive behavior therapy.* Washington, DC: American Psychological Association.

Groth-Marnat, G. (1997). *Handbook of psychological assessment.* New York: Wiley

Johnston, D. W., & Johnston, M. (2001). *Comprehensive clinical psychology.* Amsterdam: Elsevier

Reichenberg, Lourie W., & Seligman, Linda. (2016). *Selecting Effective Treatments.* A Comprehensive Systematic Guide to Treating Mental Disorders, Hoboken, NJ: Wiley

Rosenthal, H. (2006). *Therapy's best:* Practical advice and gems of wisdom from twenty accomplished counselors and therapists. New York: Haworth Press

Roth, A., Fonagy, P., (2005). *What Works for Whom?* Second Edition; A Critical Review of Psychotherapy Research, NY: Guilford Press

|

CPSIA information can be obtained
at www.ICGtesting.com
Printed in the USA
LVHW021840101218
599931LV00016B/624/P

9 780692 161722